P9-CMD-866

A Day in the Life: Desert Animals

Arabian Oryx

Anita Ganeri

Heinemann
LIBRARY
Chicago, Illinois

www.heinemannraintree.com
Visit our website to find out more information about Heinemann-Raintree books.

To order:
☎ Phone 888-454-2279
🖥 Visit www.heinemannraintree.com to browse our catalog and order online.

Edited by Daniel Nunn, Rebecca Rissman, and Sian Smith
Designed by Richard Parker
Picture research by Elizabeth Alexander
Production by Victoria Fitzgerald
Originated by Capstone Global Library Ltd
Printed and bound in the United States of America, North Mankato, MN

14 13 12
10 9 8 7 6 5 4 3 2

Library of Congress Cataloging-in-Publication Data
Ganeri, Anita, 1961–
  Arabian oryx / Anita Ganeri.
    p. cm. — (A day in the life. Desert animals)
  Includes bibliographical references and index.
  ISBN 978-1-4329-4769-9 (hc)
  ISBN 978-1-4329-4778-1 (pb)
1. Arabian oryx—Juvenile literature. I. Title.
  QL737.U53G35 2011
  599.64'5—dc22   2010022817

072012
006776RP

Acknowledgments

We would like to thank the following for permission to reproduce photographs: Alamy pp. 14 (© Photoshot Holdings Ltd), 20, 23 glossary jackal (© Robert Harding Picture Library Ltd), 22, 23 glossary hooves (© imagebroker); Ardea.com pp. 4, 23 glossary mammal, 23 glossary desert (© Richard Porter), 15, 23 glossary grazing (© Ken Lucas), 11 (© Francois Gohier); Corbis pp. 13 (© George D. Lepp), 17, 23 glossary herd (© Steve Kaufman); FLPA pp. 7 (© Philip Perry), 10 (© Inga Spence); Nature Picture Library p. 12 (© Hanne & Jens Eriksen); NHPA p. 21 (Biosphoto); Photolibrary pp. 8, 9, 19, 23 glossary scrapes (Juniors Bildarchiv), 18 (Mauritius/Kerstin Layer), 16 (Mike Hill/OSF); Shutterstock p. 5, 23 glossary springbok (© Johan Swanepoel).

Front cover photograph of an Arabian oryx standing in sand (Oryx leucoryx) reproduced with permission of Alamy (© Juniors Bildarchiv).

Back cover photograph of (left) Arabian oryx walking in sand reproduced with permission of Photolibrary (Juniors Bildarchiv); and (right) herd of Arabian oryx in Sir Bani Yas Island, United Arab Emirates, reproduced with permission of Photolibrary (Mike Hill/OSF).

We would like to thank Michael Bright for his assistance in the preparation of this book.

Every effort has been made to contact copyright holders of material reproduced in this book. Any omissions will be rectified in subsequent printings if notice is given to the publisher.

All the Internet addresses (URLs) given in this book were valid at the time of going to press. However, due to the dynamic nature of the Internet, some addresses may have changed, or sites may have changed or ceased to exist since publication. While the author and publisher regret any inconvenience this may cause readers, no responsibility for any such changes can be accepted by either the author or the publisher.

Contents

Some words are shown in bold, **like this**.
You can find them in the glossary on page 23.

What Is an Arabian Oryx?

An Arabian oryx is a **mammal**.

All mammals have some hair on their bodies and feed their babies milk.

springbok

Arabian oryxes belong to a group of mammals called antelopes.

Springboks are another type of antelope.

Where Are Arabian Oryxes Live?

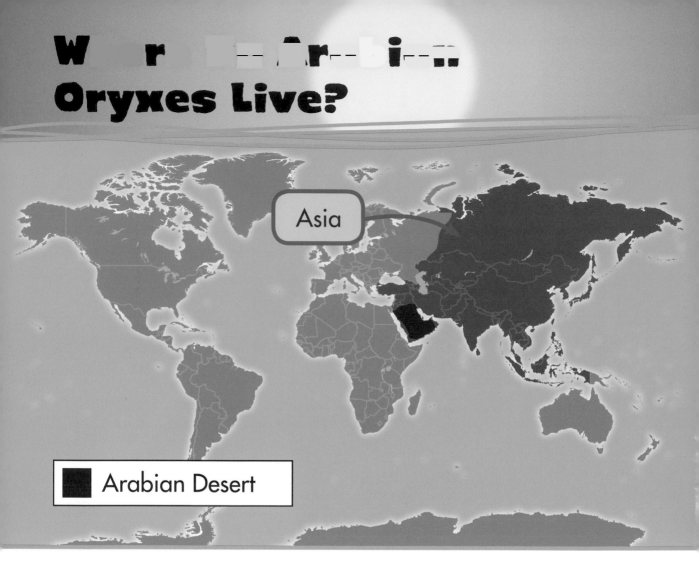

Asia

Arabian Desert

Arabian oryxes live in the Arabian **Desert** in Asia.

Can you find this desert on the map?

In summer it is very hot in the desert, but it can be freezing cold during winter nights.

There is very little rain in the desert.

What Do Arabian Oryxes Look Like?

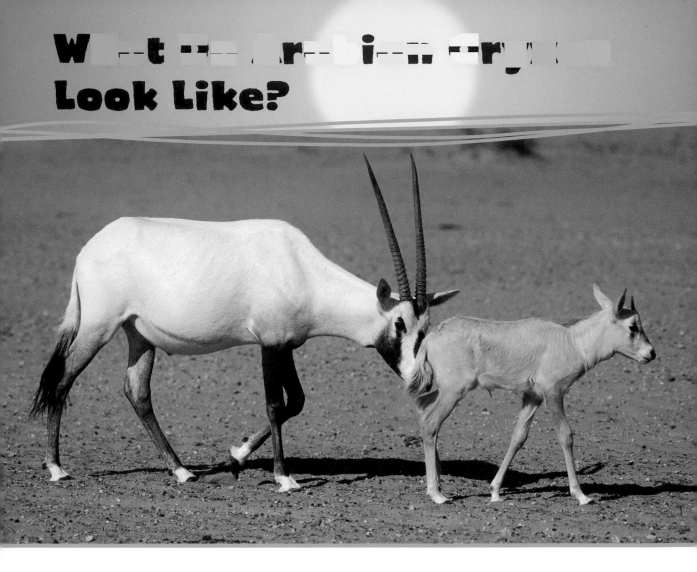

Adult Arabian oryxes are white, with brown legs.

Baby oryxes are brown all over when they are very young.

horns

hooves

Arabian oryxes have long, sharp horns.

Their wide **hooves** help them to walk across soft sand without sinking.

What Do Arabian Oryxes Do at Night?

Arabian oryxes usually start looking for food in the evening.

They spend most of the night **grazing**.

10

In the morning, it starts to get very hot in the **desert**.

The oryxes find somewhere shady to lie down and rest.

What Do Arabian Oryxes Eat?

Arabian oryxes mostly eat grass and other **desert** plants.

They feed on roots, flowers, and leaves.

Arabian oryxes can go for weeks without drinking water.

They get most of their water from the plants they eat.

Do Arabian Oryxes Stay in One Place?

The **desert** is too dry for many plants to grow.

So some nights, the oryxes have to walk long distances to find their food.

The oryxes sometimes walk to places where it has been raining.

The rain makes new plants grow for the oryxes to eat.

Do Arabian Oryxes Live Alone?

Arabian oryxes live in family groups, called **herds**.

There are usually around six oryxes in a herd.

When the oryxes move around, one of the females takes the lead.

The young follow behind with the male.

What Do Arabian Oryxes Do During the Day?

During the day, the **desert** gets very hot.

The oryxes stop feeding and look for a patch of grass or sand.

scrapes

The oryxes use their **hooves** to dig dips in the sand, called **scrapes**.

Then they lie down and rest until the evening.

What Hunts Arabian Oryxes?

Jackals hunt and eat baby oryxes.

A few oryxes are hunted by people, who eat their meat and use their skins for leather.

Arabian oryxes died out in the wild because so many were killed by hunters.

Some oryxes were born in zoos and put back into the wild.

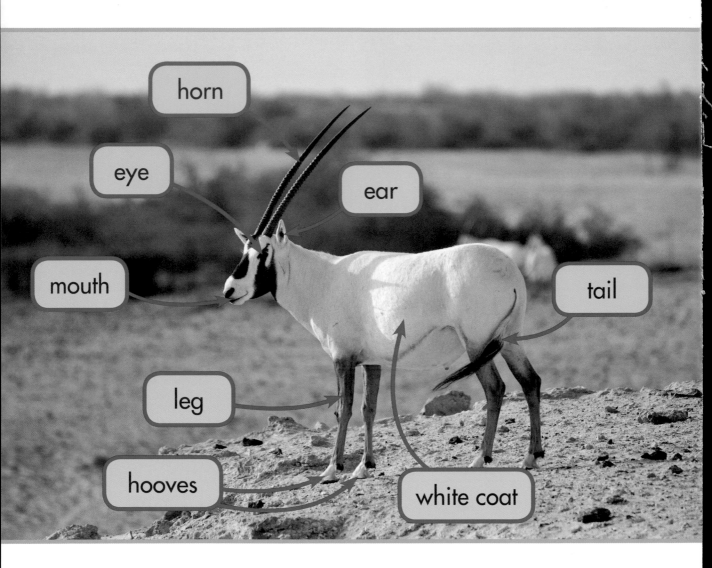

horn

eye

ear

mouth

tail

leg

hooves

white coat

 **desert** very dry place that is rocky, stony, or sandy

 **grazing** feeding on grass and other plants

 **herd** group of oryxes

 **hooves** hard outer coverings on an oryx's feet

 **jackal** dog-like animal that hunts oryxes

 **mammal** animal that feeds its babies milk. All mammals have some hair or fur on their bodies.

 **scrapes** dips that oryxes dig in the ground

 **springbok** type of antelope

Find Out More

Books

Haldane, Elizabeth. *Desert: Around the Clock with the Animals of the Desert* (24 Hours). New York: Dorling Kindersley, 2006.

Hodge, Deborah. *Desert Animals* (Who Lives Here?). Toronto: Kids Can, 2008.

MacAulay, Kelley, and Bobbie Kalman. *Desert Habitat* (Introducing Habitats). New York: Crabtree, 2008.

Websites

Look at photos of Arabian oryxes and find out about them at:
www.sandiegozoo.org/animalbytes/t-oryx.html

Learn more about Arabian oryxes at: www.phoenixzoo.org/learn/animals/animal_detail.aspx?FACT_SHEET_ID=100003

Index